UN
COMPLICATED

FAITH FOR THE REST OF US

JUSTICE COLEMAN

Published by

FMP ©2017
Foursquare Missions Press

IN
TRO

I was so excited when my friend Jake finally agreed to come with me to church. We had been friends for a year and hung out almost every week, but he always turned down my invitation with an excuse. When he finally said "yes" I was so pumped I had to literally hide my excitement and play it off cool as not to scare him. This was a big deal. I cared about Jake. God was changing my life in amazing ways and I wanted him to have the same experience.

The day finally arrived and I wasn't totally sure if Jake would show up, so I waited for him outside. When he walked up I could immediately tell he was uncomfortable. He was wearing an awkwardly long flannel shirt with the sleeves pulled down to cover all his tattoos. I did my best to joke around with him and get him to relax, but I could tell he already felt like he didn't belong.

That was the moment I began to see things from Jake's point of view. And faith was starting to look complicated.

He hugged people he had never met.

He sang songs he had never heard. (I think one of them was about a lamb.)

He listened to a sermon about a book he had never read.

And I'm pretty sure he will never look at crackers and juice the same way again.

When church was over Jake turned to me, "I need a cigarette."

Honestly, I was a little exhausted too. I had desperately wanted this day to go so well for my friend and I had just spent the last two hours leaning over his shoulder trying to explain all the nuances to make it less confusing.

Jake never came to church with me again.

Let me be clear, I am not blaming the church. I believe in the church. I pastor a church! This not a book about how to "do church." This isn't a book with all the answers and it certainly isn't a comprehensive study of systematic theology. This is simply a guide to help anyone who has ever felt left out, confused or overwhelmed by faith. I wrote this book as an attempt to help un-complicate any of those big questions.

I wrote this book for the "Jakes."

DOES GOD HAVE A PLAN?

I remember when I got my first smart phone and went on a downloading frenzy, picking out cool games and apps. I found one I thought would be helpful because it would update me with worldwide news coverage. The only problem was an alert on that app that I didn't know how to turn off, and every time I would pick up my phone a notification would be waiting for me on the home screen.

This just in:

"National poll shows divorce rate among millennials is on the climb."

"The world economy continues to decline and unemployment is up by X percent."

"Recent terrorist attack leaves 100 dead and 30 missing."

It felt like every time I reached for my phone, I read

another story about how the world was only getting worse. Maybe I shouldn't admit this, but eventually I just deleted that app. I don't think I was prepared to be aware of all the *hell* that was going on around me.

Brokenness is all around us. If we were to take a plate and drop it on the floor, it would shatter into dozens of pieces. Brokenness, by its very nature, tells us a story. Each piece points back to a time of wholeness, when it connected to something bigger than itself. It was once complete. In the same way, we can look at our world today and see broken pieces all around us. What do those pieces say? What story do they tell? Does God have a plan?

The story of God starts with love. He created the world to be healthy and whole and to experience His love. The relationship that mankind had with God was powerful and personal. Creator God breathed His own breath into mankind to give them life. With that Spirit power He said,

"Be fruitful and multiply. Fill the earth and govern it. Reign over the fish in the sea, the birds in the sky, and all the animals that scurry along the ground." (Genesis 1:28)

This was God's plan: to partner with mankind as a co-creator and to develop the world into something incredible and full of His love. The plan started off well, but somewhere along the way man believed a different story. He believed a lie that his plans were better than God's plan. Through his disobedience, he introduced sin into the world.

Sin, by definition, is to do what you know is wrong or to not do what you know is right.

In many ways, sin is like a virus that was introduced to a healthy world and infects us in three primary relationships:

1. **Sin is a virus in our relationship with God.** God is holy and sin puts a distance between us and His holiness. Our infection has essentially quarantined us from our Creator.

2. **Sin is a virus in our relationship with other people.** The virus manifests itself in selfishness and fear and infects the way we treat others. When we always put ourselves first, we neglect the best interest of others.

3. **Sin is a virus in our relationship with the world.** Whether it is violence, corruption, war or climate change, you don't need a smart phone app to know who is responsible. The world has man's fingerprints all over it.

2,000 years ago, God looked at the world and said, "They are never going to be able to put things back together. If I leave them to themselves and to their sin, they will remain helpless, broken, hurting and suffering." So God sent His son Jesus.

For God so loved the world that he gave his one and only Son, that whoever believes in him shall not perish but have eternal life. For God did not send his Son into the world to condemn the world, but to save the world through him. (John 3:16-17 NIV)

In many ways, Jesus is an "antivirus" to the infection we are experiencing. Creation is sick, but because of Jesus, we can be free of the sin-virus and restored to a right relationship with God, each other and the world.

Three ways that only Jesus is qualified as an antivirus:

1. **An antivirus must originate from outside of the system.** He left heaven to come to earth as fully God and fully human.

2. **An antivirus must be incorruptible.** Jesus lived a life that was sinless and blameless, demonstrating His strength against the virus and its effects.

3. **An antivirus must be powerful enough to absorb and replace the existing infection.** Jesus' resurrection from death shows us His power to absorb our sin and to give us a new life filled with His Spirit.

Can you imagine a life where the sin-virus is no longer infecting our relationship with God, each other and the world?

Imagine if sin didn't come between you and the holiness of God. What would your relationship with Him look like? What would stop you from discovering His purpose for your life?

Imagine if sin didn't infect your relationship with your family and friends. What would a love-centered life look like instead of a self-centered life? Could love truly replace bitterness and unforgiveness?

Imagine if sin wasn't infecting the world. What would it look like if God's people worked together to address the injustices and pain of this world and truly work toward a cure?

Imagine that He chose you for this plan.

Maybe you live in a world that is constantly telling you that it is falling apart. The good news is that God does have a plan. He has had the same plan since the beginning of time. He wants to partner with His people to create a world that would truly know Him and experience His love. God wants to change the world.

He just doesn't want to do it without you.

Discussion Questions

If sin is like a virus, in what ways has it infected our relationship with God, each other, and the world? Does God have a plan? In what way does Jesus fulfill that plan?

UNcomplicate It

Are there areas of your life in need of a cure? If so, what are some of those areas?

WHAT IS DISCIPLE-SHIP?

Matthew, Mark, Luke and John are four books in the Bible that chronicle the life of Jesus and His ministry. Each account is told by a different author with a different perspective, but the ministry of Jesus always starts off the same way — He recruits 12 disciples.

Disciple isn't a word that we use very much in the 21st century, but, basically, Jesus was choosing His apprentices. He hand-picked 12 guys with the intention of training them up to help Him with ministry and eventually carry on the mission beyond His time on earth. Though this arrangement may be slightly foreign to us, the rabbi/disciple relationship was clear to the disciples. For the most part, the disciples knew what they were getting themselves into. Rabbis didn't just choose students; they chose *future rabbis.*

During three years of training, the disciples were fully immersed in the life of Jesus. They hardly left His side. When a blind man received sight for the very first time, the disciples were the first people he saw. When a paralyzed man got up and started jumping around, they jumped around with him. When the little girl came back to life at her funeral and sat up in her casket, the disciples were sitting front row. Or, maybe they ran away screaming . . . I'm not sure, that is pretty freaky.

Not only did they witness the craziest miracles you can imagine, they participated in them. Jesus gave the disciples power to do everything He was doing and sent them out to preach and to heal the sick. This was an apprenticeship on steroids!

Here is the interesting part . . .

As we read through their discipleship journey, it doesn't take long to realize that they didn't have it all figured out. Despite the incredibly close relationship they had with Jesus, they still couldn't connect all the dots. So Jesus pulls them aside and asks them a question:

"Who do you say that I am?"

"Well," they replied, *"some say John the Baptist, some say Elijah, and others say Jeremiah or one of the other prophets back from the dead."*

Jesus responded, "I'm not asking what they say, I'm asking what you say. Who do you say that I am?"

Can we stop right there? Why was it so hard for the disciples to give Jesus a straight answer? These guys have spent day and night with Jesus for over a year at this point. Nobody knew Jesus better than His disciples. There is no one more qualified to answer this question. So why was it so hard?

Finally, Peter courageously pipes up, **"You are the Christ, the son of God."**

In the next scene, Jesus takes Peter and two other disciples on a hiking trip to the top of a mountain. I wonder what was going through their minds.

"Why did He choose us? What is He training us for? What is at the top of this mountain?"

When Peter, James and John reach the top, they witness something so incredible, they will never look at their Rabbi the same way again.

Jesus transfigures before them.

Almost without warning, His eyes, face and clothes become brighter than the sun. The glory of God bursts from within Him and the disciples fall to the ground, blinded. It is so mind blowing that Jesus has to comfort them,

"Do not be afraid."

The disciples were truly in the presence of God.

Transfiguration is another word we don't use that often. It comes from the Greek word that means metamorphosis. Jesus didn't take the disciples up to a mountain to show them that He could turn into God. That is not what is happening here. Jesus is revealing that He has always been God. Before time began, at the creation of the world, Jesus was there because He is God. He left heaven to come to earth in the form of a man so that He could reach humanity on our level. But He never stopped being God.

This may be the first time the disciples were at the top of this mountain, but this wasn't the first time they were in the presence of God. God had been with them the whole time. They just didn't realize it until now.

It is important to understand the difference between *conforming* and *transforming.* When something conforms, it changes into something other than itself. Transformation is the opposite, it is the process of becoming something new without compromising what it has always been.

The Greek word for transfigure is used another time in scripture. But it is not about Jesus. It is about anyone who accepts the invitation to be His disciple.

Do not be conformed to this world, but be transformed by the renewing of your mind, that you may prove what is that good and acceptable and perfect will of God. (Romans 12:2 NKJV)

God is not interested in changing you into something other than yourself. He doesn't want you to conform into anything at all, certainly not into the ways of this world. He likes the way He made you. That is why He created you.

The transfiguration shows us that God's will is less about where we are going, and more about who we are becoming. Your journey as a disciple will be full of mountains and valleys, and God can use any one of them to reveal Himself to you, shape your character and transform your life.

Discipleship is a transforming relationship with Jesus that will take you beyond a mountain top experience and into the fullness of who He has created you to be. When all you know is conformity, your focus is limited to what waits for you at the top. But the same God you are looking for has been journeying with you the whole time.

It is not the top of the mountain that is special, it is the Rabbi you are following along the trail.

2

Discussion Questions

What is the difference between conforming and transforming?

In your experience, do you tend to give more attention to *where you are going or who you are becoming*?

UNcomplicate It

Recognizing that you are in a personal process of transformation, what would a practical stage of metamorphosis look like in your life? How is God growing you?

WHAT IS THE BIBLE?

When most people think of Southern California, I imagine they picture an ocean breeze and palm trees lining every block. While growing up, I spent plenty of time in the ocean, but our block didn't have any palm trees — every yard in our neighborhood had orange trees. We even had a full orange grove just a couple streets over. Needless to say, my mom never brought home oranges from the market. We just went outside and picked them for ourselves.

It wasn't until my first year of marriage that I actually bought fruit at a grocery store. I remember washing an orange in the sink when I noticed something I'd never seen before: the orange appeared to be two-toned. One side was a fresh vibrant color and the other side looked yellow like an old sponge. A quick Google search confirmed my suspicion. Someone had spray painted that orange! The FDA has actually approved a colorant called "Citrus Red No. 2" that can be sprayed on fruit to dye the skin a different color. The outer layer had been modified to give the appearance that it was healthy and ripe.

No good tree bears bad fruit, nor does a bad tree bear good fruit. A tree is identified by its fruit. (Luke 6:43-44 NIV)

That's the thing about fruit trees, and I've seen a lot of them, you can't really tell much just by looking at them. In fact, you can examine a tree all day long — measure the trunk, shake the branches, examine the bark — but at the end of the day, only the fruit from that tree will tell you what you want to know: how does the fruit taste? I've seen plenty of trees that look great on the outside, but, season after season, produce fruit that I just don't want to bring in my house.

When I decided to follow Jesus, it felt like God replanted my life. I moved away to a Christian college in a new city and away from my friends and family. I have to admit, having to make all new friends was pretty lonely. Even though it was hard, I am so grateful for those first couple months, because that is when I decided to give the Bible a shot. What I discovered not only fascinated me, it changed my life.

Over the span of 1600 years, God used over 40 different people to write the 66 books that would become the Bible. Kings, peasants, farmers, fishermen, poets, war heroes, were all inspired by God as the Author to write what has become the best selling book of all time. Every year, nothing even comes close to out-selling the Bible. This is probably because it has been translated into over 1200 different languages and dialects. That means, currently, over 90% of the world can read the Bible in their own language. Maybe that is why the Bible is not only the best selling book of all time, it is also the most stolen book of all time!

I remember one of the first stories I read as a new Christian: Jesus was tempted by the devil in the wilderness when He was all alone. It immediately jumped out to me, because I felt in some strange way like I was alone in a wilderness of sorts.

Jesus, full of the Holy Spirit, left the Jordan and was led by the Spirit into the wilderness, where for forty days he was tempted by the devil. He ate nothing during those days, and at the end of them he was hungry.

The devil said to him, "If you are the Son of God, tell this stone to become bread." (Luke 4:1-3 NIV)

But Jesus told him, "No! The Scriptures say, 'People do not live by bread alone, but by every word that comes from the mouth of God.'" (Luke 4:4)

I don't know if you caught that, but the devil waited until Jesus was at His most vulnerable moment before he tempted Him. Jesus had gone forty days without food and He was starving, exhausted, physically stressed, weak and alone. How did Jesus respond?

He answered with the Bible. The enemy tempts Him two more times, and guess what? Each time, Jesus responds with scriptures that He has committed to memory. Let that sink in for a minute.

Jesus is God and He still leans on the Bible for strength.

The Bible is unlike anything else ever written. It stands in a category unto itself. It is not just a fascinating best seller or a great book of wisdom. It changes lives because it changes hearts. The Bible is not something we add to our spiritual life. It is God's way of preparing our spiritual life.

All Scripture is inspired by God and is useful to teach us what is true and to make us realize what is wrong in our lives. It corrects us when we are wrong and teaches us to do what is right. God uses it to prepare and equip his people to do every good work. (2 Timothy 3:16-17)

Just like with Jesus, there are seasons of testing and temptation in our lives. Usually they find us in our weakest moments . . . when we are tired, alone, stressed, and running on empty.

With enough practice, we can keep the outer layer looking vibrant and ripe, but it doesn't take long before something eventually pierces the skin. What lies beneath the peel? What happens when life gives you the squeeze? What will come pouring out?

The question isn't if the tree has fruit or not. The question is if it's sweet or sour.

Discussion Questions

In your experience, how has reading the scriptures impacted your faith?

Has there ever been a time in your life when you were depleted, under stress or lost and the Bible helped guide you?

UNcomplicate It

Share a time you were surprised by your own sourness or sweetness.

WHO IS GOD THE FATHER?

If I had to describe my dad in two words, they would be "hard working." Growing up, I watched him run a business as a contractor who wasn't afraid to take on tough projects. He didn't mess around when it came to getting the job done, finding a solution or getting his hands dirty. There was always work to be done on weekends and summer breaks, and that meant I could work with him and earn extra money for a new skateboard or video game.

I actually loved working with my pops, not only because I loved spending time with him, but because I love spending time with power tools! He had every tool you could imagine and I was his little helper.

Jesus grew up working construction with His earthly dad, too. Even though we don't have very many stories about His life before He went into ministry, we know that He was a carpenter and worked the family business until He transitioned into ministry. One day,

He was "working" on the Sabbath, which according to the religious law was a holy day, when no work was allowed.

So the Jewish leaders began harassing Jesus for breaking the Sabbath rules. But Jesus replied, "My Father is always working, and so am I."

So the Jewish leaders tried all the harder to find a way to kill him. For he not only broke the Sabbath, he called God his Father, thereby making himself equal with God.

So Jesus explained, "I tell you the truth, the Son can do nothing by himself. He does only what he sees the Father doing. Whatever the Father does, the Son also does." (John 5:16-19)

Maybe for Jesus, doing miracles on the Sabbath was a grey area. Was that really considered "work" for Him? It's not like the Old Testament law of God had an outline of when to do miracles and divine healings. So, He looked to His Father as an example and what did He see Him doing?

Working.

I have three kids, and my oldest boy likes to work with me too. Well, sometimes he doesn't want to help, so I just start making a lot of noise with my power tools and he comes running. When he was three years old, we got him a little plastic tool set complete with a hammer, screw driver and electric drill. It actually looked just like mine and was battery powered. He loved it.

One time, I was standing on a ladder in our kitchen using my electric drill above my head to mount something to the wall, and I will never forget what I saw when I looked down. My son had his drill raised above his head, pressed against the wall, copying my every move. It caught me completely by surprise. I didn't even realize he was there. I guess he didn't know what to do, so he just did what he saw his father doing.

That is going to happen. There will be times in your life when you won't know what to do. There will be times you just don't know what is the right or wrong, and times you don't know left or right. God designed it that way because it requires faith. And it requires knowing God as your Father.

God could have picked a million different ways to relate to us as created beings, but He chose to be our Father. When you look to God, He wants you to see Him as your Heavenly Father. His desire is that your relationship with Him would be like a loving dad with his son or daughter. God can take on a lot of roles in your life, if you let Him. He can be your provider, teacher, healer, king . . . but what He wants most of all is to be your Loving Father.

One time, my son was playing in the backyard with the neighborhood kids, jumping on the trampoline and making lots of noise. I was in the house working on a project, but I kept the back sliding door open so

I could hear them. Suddenly, everything went quiet. Every parent knows that loud noises are to be expected. It's when things go quiet that usually something out of the ordinary is happening. I walked out to the backyard to check things out and the neighbors were already grabbing their things and on their way home.

"What happened?" I asked my son.

He just stood there on the trampoline, by himself, with his head down. I don't remember what happened, or why he thought he was in trouble, but I will never forget that look on his face.

Guilt.

"What happened, Son?" I asked again.

He didn't answer. He couldn't. He wanted to tell me, but it was like he was stuck. Then suddenly, he ran and dove into my arms. He didn't talk at first, he just wanted to hug. But after I asked a few questions, he "fessed up" and explained what happened.

What if you had a Heavenly Father who you could go to with anything? What if He was so loving and trustworthy that even when you made mistakes, disobeyed or totally screwed up, your first instincts were to run to Him and dive into His arms? That is what God wants as your Father.

And that is how you know that guilt is not from God.

Guilt is the worst feeling in the world. It makes you want to look down, hide your face and even run away. Your Heavenly Father would never do anything to push you away from Him. His greatest desire for your life is that you would experience His love and never choose anything over being close with Him. Just like a child growing up, you are going to make mistakes and you are going to sin. Even though God hates sin, He loves you. Your sin doesn't catch Him by surprise.

But God showed his great love for us by sending Christ to die for us while we were still sinners. (Romans 5:8)

You have a Heavenly Father who has done everything He can to show His love to you. Don't let guilt separate you from Him. Guilt may make you want to run *away,* but run *toward* Him instead.

Dive into the arms of your Father.

And, if you get lost . . . just look to Jesus, because He only does what He sees the Father doing.

Discussion Questions

How do we know that God doesn't give guilt trips?

Have you ever wanted to make the right choice, but found it wasn't as black and white as you thought?

UNcomplicate It

Share a story from your childhood when you got in trouble with a parent. How did you respond? What can you observe now about your behavior?

WHO IS GOD THE SON?

On my 11th birthday, I received the coolest gift of my entire life — my very own snowboard! This was back in the day when skiers ruled the mountain and snowboards were just making their way onto the scene. My snowboard was awesome! It looked like something out of an 80's skateboard magazine. I'll never forget the sweet purple design and the big green lightning bolt across the front. It screamed, "EXTREME!" There was a little ski resort just an hour from our house that only had two lifts, but it was the perfect place to practice for the X-Games.

One day, near the end of the season, I guess I had gotten the hang of riding and carving a little bit, because I noticed a little jump over in the shade. I had never tried a jump before, but this one was small and not too scary. So I lined myself up, and headed straight toward the ramp of packed snow.

What I didn't see was the patch of ice.

What you may not realize is that a snowboard can't slow down when it is on top of ice. Snowboards maneuver by "carving," which is basically building resistance against the edge of the board like a snow plow. You can't plow ice, you can only slide.

I remember the instant regret of trying to pull a fast stop at the top of the jump, and my feet flying out from underneath me. The crash was so bad that the binding that attached my boot to the board actually ripped out. My body felt broken and my snowboard was in pieces. As devastating and painful as that was, I eventually had to pick myself up and walk down the mountain, board in hand. It may have been my last run that day, but it wasn't my last time on a snowboard.

John wrote his Gospel for people who were interested in learning about Jesus. Most of them did not come from a Jewish background and he wanted them to start with the basics. You may have noticed that his account includes different miracles than the other three books, and events seem to be in a slightly different order. Matthew, Mark and Luke all start with Jesus' life on earth, His parents and His birth. When John wrote his Gospel, he wanted to start at the beginning . . . the very beginning.

In the beginning the Word already existed. The Word was with God, and the Word was God. (John 1:1)

John calls Jesus "the Word" because he is writing in the Greek language to an audience with a Greco-

Roman worldview. *Logos,* translated "the Word," brilliantly explains that Jesus is not only God's Son, but He is fully God who is present at creation. It is important to know that Jesus didn't become God. He has always been God. When Jesus was in human form, He was 100% God and 100% man at the same time. He wasn't half God and half man . . . that would be Hercules.

The Word became flesh and made his dwelling among us. We have seen his glory, the glory of the one and only Son, who came from the Father, full of grace and truth. (John 1:14 NIV)

Jesus fully embodies both the grace and truth of God. We see this in His divine and human nature. The humanity of Jesus shows us God's unbelievable grace, that He would come to this earth to live a sinless life and willingly give Himself as a substitute for our sin. Jesus took the punishment on the cross that we deserve.

Equally so, the divine nature of God establishes the truth. There is nothing we can ever do to earn that kind of love from God. Salvation is a gift and can only be received as such. We don't deserve new life — we deserve death.

God saved you by his grace when you believed. And you can't take credit for this; it is a gift from God. Salvation is not a reward for the good things we have done, so none of us can boast about it. (Ephesians 2:8-9)

Grace and truth are kind of like the two edges to a snowboard. There is a toe-side edge and a heel-side edge, and they are equally important. You need both to experience snowboarding to the fullest. When someone is first learning, they usually have a proclivity toward one edge or the other. For some it is more natural to kick out and dig their heels in, but for others it feels right to turn in the other way onto their toes.

One side is not more important than the other, but one side always feels more natural.

It is the same way with grace and truth. Each of us tends to lean more one way or the other. When someone leans heavy on the truth side, they often see life as black and white. God is holy and we are sinners. God gave His life for us, so we give our life for Him. But just like a snowboard, if you stay on one edge too long, you start to go sideways.

"I screwed up again, I can't believe it! How can God possibly forgive me this time? I'm not worthy of His love."

Without grace we are left to the piercing truth of God's holiness. We don't deserve a second chance because we never deserved a first chance! It is the grace of God made evident in Jesus that keeps us in His arms and reminds us of His everlasting love.

But if we confess our sins to him, he is faithful and just to forgive us our sins and to cleanse us from all wickedness. If we claim we have not

sinned, we are calling God a liar and showing that his word has no place in our hearts. (1 John 1:9-10)

Always riding the grace edge, with no balance of truth, can be equally as unhealthy and dangerous. When someone only leans on grace, there is often no desire to change their life or grow. To neglect the truth of God is to ignore the reality of the price He paid for us.

"Oh, it's OK. Even though I know what I am doing is wrong, God will forgive me."

God accepts you just the way you are, but He loves you too much to let you stay that way. Jesus is the visible picture of the invisible God. It is because of His life that we know what God is like, and we can know His character as our example.

No matter where you find yourself on the mountain, sitting on the bunny slopes or tackling black diamonds, there are only two edges to that snowboard. Both sides are equally important to knowing the fullness of God that is present in the person and the work of Jesus. Grace and truth are truly the gatekeepers to experiencing life to the fullness.

And keep an eye out for ice patches, of course.

Discussion Questions

How does Jesus embody both grace and truth, equally?

In your own life, does grace or truth come more naturally? Which way do you tend to lean?

UNcomplicate It

Name an area in your life that you need to give yourself more grace or more truth.

WHO IS GOD THE HOLY SPIRIT?

A few years back, I had the incredible opportunity to visit Israel and take a boat out on the Sea of Galilee. It was amazing to be on the same lake where so many miracles took place and Jesus walked on water. What amazed me the most was the size of this enormous body of water. The modern name for it is *Lake* Kinneret, and Luke refers to it in his gospel as *Lake* Tiberius, because this huge body of water is technically a lake surrounded on all sides by land and mountains. Locals started calling it the *Sea* of Galilee because of its ocean-like reputation for storms. Winds traveling through the mountains shoot down across the water quickly, creating dangerous waves that feel like an ocean. The lake is infamous for storms that seem to come out of nowhere and there are plenty of boats at the bottom of it because fishermen set sail on a lake, but weren't prepared for a sea.

There is a pretty scary story around the time Jesus first recruits His disciples. They all get in a boat and He tells them to head across to the other side. It is the middle of the night and the wind begins to blow stronger and the waves begin to grow larger. Before long, the disciples find themselves waist deep in a furious storm.

Suddenly, a fierce storm struck the lake, with waves breaking into the boat. But Jesus was sleeping. The disciples went and woke him up, shouting, "Lord, save us! We're going to drown!" Jesus responded, "Why are you afraid? You have so little faith!" Then he got up and rebuked the wind and waves, and suddenly there was a great calm.

The disciples were amazed. "Who is this man?" they asked. "Even the winds and waves obey him!" (Matthew 8:24-27)

Quite a few of Jesus's disciples were former fishermen. They had navigated these waters before, but there was something eerie about this storm. Not only did it seem to come out of nowhere, it almost seemed personal . . . like it was attacking them and trying to sink them.

Imagine a small boat being tossed by the waves as the crew scrambles around yelling at each other over the howling wind. Wave after wave comes crashing into the boat and it fills with water to the point of almost capsizing.

And Jesus was sleeping? If you ask me, that is the eerie part.

"Lord, save us! We're going to drown!"

The only thing scarier than being in the middle of a storm and thinking you are going to die is when your Rabbi wakes up from His nap, stands up and at the sound of His command, it all stops.

The wind instantly stops blowing, the waves go flat, the boat stops rocking . . . everything goes quiet. No one says a word.

"Why are you afraid? You have so little faith!"

"Little faith" in Greek is actually one word combined of two parts. It doesn't mean *small* in size, as if compared to something larger. It means *immature* in size, like it is underdeveloped — similar to a baby that is still growing up.

Jesus not only rebukes the storm. He rebukes the disciples.

I have to admit, this part is a little hard to read. What were the disciples supposed to do? The storm was raging and the boat was sinking, so they ran to Jesus for help. And Jesus rebukes them for that? How many times am I overwhelmed in life and feel like I am about to drown, so I run to Jesus for help? I thought that was what we were supposed to do.

The next line gives it away.

"Who is this man?" they asked.

Suddenly it all makes sense. It becomes clear when you see their reaction. "Who is this man?" The disciples were looking at Jesus like He was only a man. They didn't see Him as God. They were only fearing for their life because they didn't realize Who was in their boat!

Life isn't supposed to be scary when Jesus is in your boat. How do you think it makes God the Father feel when He sees His kids living in fear? I can tell you as a father myself, He hates it. It is a terrible feeling to see someone you love scared and afraid. God knows that life is scary, you don't know when the next storm is going to spring up and waves will come crashing into your boat. That is why He gives us the Holy Spirit, who is the presence of God. It is not enough to know who God is, He wants to dwell within you.

Jesus explained this to His disciples the night before He died. He called everyone together for their last meal to help them understand that just because He was physically leaving earth, that didn't mean they would be alone.

And I will pray the Father, and He will give you another Helper, that He may abide with you forever - the Spirit of truth, whom the world cannot receive, because it neither sees Him nor knows Him; but you know Him, for He dwells with you and will be in you. (John 14:16-17 NKJV)

God the Holy Spirit is the presence of God who lives

in you and works through you. The disciples didn't understand this at first, but they would soon discover that the Holy Spirit would be a constant relationship and presence in their life. He would help them, just like Jesus had, by comforting, leading them to truth and giving them power.

God never designed you to live in fear. You were made for faith. Faith is access to the life God has for you, and fear will only hold you back.

There is no fear in love. But perfect love drives out fear . . . (1 John 4:18 NIV)

God's desire is that nothing would hold you back from the life He has for you. Storms will come and try to shake your boat, but He wants to fill you with His presence and power, so that no matter how big the waves, your confidence is in Him. There is nothing to fear. God is on your side.

He is in your boat.

Maybe it is time to take a nap.

6

Discussion Questions

Why do you think Jesus rebuked His disciples before He rebuked the wind and the waves?

Are there areas in your life where you feel afraid or not in control? Is it possible for these areas to be opportunities to strengthen your faith?

UNcomplicate It

Jesus promised that even though He would not be with them physically, they could have a personal relationship with God the Holy Spirit. Have you experienced the gift of this relationship? If so, describe how this has changed your life.

WHAT IS PRAYER?

Martial arts has always been a big part of my life. My parents probably enrolled me, in part, because of some behavioral issues and thought the discipline would help. I've always loved training, and over the years, had the privilege of learning from some incredible teachers.

There was a season I even got to train with one of the only living grand masters of Japanese Jiu Jitsu. This man was a living legend and he disciplined his body and his spirit unlike anything I had ever seen. Every class, he would destroy our bodies with a brutal workout, but not before we had spent some time in meditation and breathing exercises. Grandmaster would always stress how important this part of our training was. He had a particular way he wanted us to sit, fold our hands and breathe.

I always struggled with this part. I don't know if it was the meditation or just the sitting still part, but the struggle was real.

One day after class, I asked Grandmaster about his disciplines at home. He told me that every morning he would get up early to stretch and meditate for hours, which is pretty much what I expected.

"How long do you stretch for?" I dared to ask.

"Two hours every day," he answered.

"Oh wow, how long do you meditate?" I risked digging deeper.

"15 minutes," said the Grandmaster.

15 minutes! A wave of relief swept over me. If he only meditates 15 minutes, and he has been doing this his whole life, then maybe I'm putting way too much pressure on myself as a white belt.

Once Jesus was in a certain place praying. As he finished, one of his disciples came to him and said, "Lord, teach us to pray, just as John taught his disciples."

Jesus said, "This is how you should pray:

Father, may your name be kept holy. May your Kingdom come soon. Give us each day the food we need and forgive us our sins, as we forgive those who sin against us. And don't let us yield to temptation." (Luke 11:1-4)

Isn't it interesting that the disciples had to ask Jesus to teach them how to pray? You would think that prayer would be a foundational first step as a disciple. How long had they been following Jesus before they brought this up to Him? A year? Is it possible they were struggling with prayer on their own and that is where this question was coming from?

Then, teaching them more about prayer, he used this story: "Suppose you went to a friend's house at midnight, wanting to borrow three loaves of bread. You say to him, 'A friend of mine has just arrived for a visit, and I have nothing for him to eat.' And suppose he calls out from his bedroom, 'Don't bother me. The door is locked for the night, and my family and I are all in bed. I can't help you.' But I tell you this—though he won't do it for friendship's sake, if you keep knocking long enough, he will get up and give you whatever you need because of your shameless persistence. And so I tell you, keep on asking, and you will receive what you ask for. Keep on seeking, and you will find. Keep on knocking, and the door will be opened to you. For everyone who asks, receives. Everyone who seeks, finds. And to everyone who knocks, the door will be opened." (Luke 11:5-10)

The disciples ask Jesus to teach them how to pray and He answers with a story about someone who just keeps knocking on a door until it opens. Sounds to me like Jesus was encouraging some disciples who felt like they weren't "doing prayer" right. I don't know about you, but this certainly encourages me.

Here are three simple things we learn from Jesus about prayer:

1. Create space to talk with God.

> *"Once Jesus was in a certain place praying. As he finished . . . "*

2. Talk to God as your Father.

"Father, may your name be kept holy."

3. Be persistent and don't be afraid to ask.

"If you keep knocking long enough, he will get up and give you whatever you need because of your shameless persistence."

As a pastor, people are often interested in how I approach God in prayer. I guess they think I know a secret that they don't. Whenever I get that question, I am reminded of the Jiu Jitsu Grandmaster and how relieved I was with his answer. In my experience, most people ask that question because they feel like they are doing something wrong. Maybe what Jesus is showing us with this story is that you can't "do prayer" wrong.

Can you knock on a door wrong?

Prayer, simply put, is your communication with God. Maybe Jesus didn't write a step by step guide on prayer because He knew that would over-complicate it. Maybe He was more interested in His followers discovering what it was like for them to connect to God in their own personal way.

Maybe He tells a story about knocking on the door so we can get our focus off of the door and onto Who is waiting for us on the other side.

Discussion Questions

How would you describe prayer in your own words?

What is the point of Jesus' story about the neighbor who wanted to borrow bread?

UNcomplicate It

The disciples found Jesus at a "certain place" praying. Do you create space to engage with God in prayer? What does that look like?

WHAT IS WORSHIP?

When I was a kid, my family loved going to church. Every Sunday, we piled into the family station wagon for Sunday morning worship and then went back again that evening for Bible study. For the most part, I liked going to church and seeing my church friends, but I also liked going out for ice cream afterward.

One Sunday, we were running late and my parents were waiting for me in the driveway. As I bolted out the front door, I heard my mom call out the car window,

"I don't think sooooo. Go back in there and put on your Sunday's best."

Maybe I forgot, or maybe I was just trying to slip by without my parents noticing, but it was obvious that I wasn't dressed appropriately for Sunday worship. In my family, Sunday was the "Lord's day" and that meant nice clothes, nice shoes and nice behavior.

On Sunday, I looked a little different. I didn't wear my regular clothes.

On Sunday, I hung out with different friends. They weren't my regular friends.

On Sunday, I talked a little different. I was extra careful to watch my mouth.

On Sunday, we tried to be the best versions of ourselves. I'm not saying we were phonies or anything close to that, we just treated Sunday special because it was the day we worshiped God. Without realizing it, the more I elevated Sunday and put it in the "worship" category, the more every other day seemed to fall into the "non-worship" category by default.

In Jesus' day, there was only one official place of worship — the temple in Jerusalem. This was the only location where sacrifices and events were held. One day, Jesus was teaching in the court of the temple when a religious leader tested Him with a question about what it means to truly love and worship God. Jesus answered in part with a story.

"A Jewish man was traveling from Jerusalem down to Jericho, and he was attacked by bandits. They stripped him of his clothes, beat him up, and left him half dead beside the road. By chance a priest came along. But when he saw the man lying there, he crossed to the other side of the road and passed him by. A Temple assistant walked over and looked at him lying there, but he also passed by on the other side. Then a despised Samaritan came along, and when he saw the

man, he felt compassion for him. Going over to him, the Samaritan soothed his wounds with olive oil and wine and bandaged them. Then he put the man on his own donkey and took him to an inn, where he took care of him. The next day he handed the innkeeper two silver coins, telling him, 'Take care of this man. If his bill runs higher than this, I'll pay you the next time I'm here.'" (Luke 10:30-35)

It sounds to me like Jesus was answering a different question. Sometimes there is a question behind the question, and that is what God is really interested in.

The religious leader was trying to get Jesus to make a separation between what is to be considered "worship," but didn't realize he was creating another category called "non-worship."

Jesus explains with this story that the worship of God is not limited to a singular place or event. Worship is found within the motives of our heart and behind every choice that we make. Ultimately, we show God we love Him by the way we love people. When the Samaritan stopped to help the man, he worshiped God with his time. When he paid for his care, he worshiped God with his money. When he carried the man on his donkey, he worshiped God with his donkey!

That's the thing about being human, we are worship beings. We are always worshiping something because our thoughts, motives and actions are always pointed to something or someone.

The question isn't *if* or *when* we are worshiping. The question is to *whom* are we worshiping?

I am so grateful that my parents raised me in church and taught me *Who* to worship. I am much older now with a family of my own and we all love church too. We are there every week. We love seeing our church friends, learning the Bible and gathering for worship. I know from experience that there is something inherently powerful about starting off the week by choosing to put God first on Sunday. My prayer is that translates into every area of my family's life and becomes our everyday attitude and posture of our heart.

The question behind the question: *If Sunday is the Lord's Day, what about the other days? How do I worship every day like it is His?*

So whether you eat or drink, or whatever you do, do it all for the glory of God. (1 Corinthians 10:31)

Discussion Questions

What was your religious/spiritual background growing up?

Is there a difference between worshiping God and following Jesus?

UNcomplicate It

Are there areas of your life that have accidentally fallen into the imaginary "non-worship" category? If so, what are some of the unseen opportunities to worship God?

WHAT IS WATER BAPTISM?

Malibu, California is home to the rich and famous and some of the most expensive real estate in the world. What is it about living near the beach that has millionaires fighting over property like it's the only place left with a view? You could ask Tony Stark, or you could just drive down Pacific Coast Highway at 6:37 pm today and I promise you will understand.

The only thing more beautiful than a sunset on the horizon is a sunset on the ocean. It doesn't matter where you're from, a sunset is one of the most breath taking views on our planet. It's more than beautiful, it's a metaphor. Some would call it a metaphor.

Some would call it a religious experience.

They who dwell in the ends of the earth stand in awe of Your signs; You make the dawn and the sunset shout for joy. (Psalm 65:8 NASB)

If you could take a time machine to any moment in

the Bible, when would it be? Would you want to see the parting of the Red Sea? What about when Jesus calmed the raging storm or walked on water? If I could time travel to any moment, I would want to witness Jesus coming out of the water.

Before Jesus began His ministry of preaching and miracles, He was water baptized in the Jordan river. There was a spiritual revolution going at the time, and thousands of people were giving their hearts back to God. They declared their faith and commitment by immersion in the water as a sign of the old life washing away and beginning anew. What an incredible sight to see so many people declaring their faith in God. When it was Jesus' turn, He didn't need to give His heart back to God, because He had never sinned. But everything changed from that moment forward.

As Jesus came up out of the water, he saw the heavens splitting apart and the Holy Spirit descending on him like a dove. And a voice from heaven said, "You are my dearly loved Son, and you bring me great joy." (Mark 1:10-11)

If I could witness any miracle in the Bible first hand, this would be it. This is one of the only places we see God the Father, Son & Holy Spirit all present at the same moment.

Would you call this a religious experience?

As a pastor, I kind of have a love/hate relationship with the word *religion.* For some people it is a word that conjures fond memories of their childhood, church or new life.

For some it is just the opposite.

Religion, by definition, is a system or process that bridges the common man with a holy God. Oftentimes it is a priest or holy man with more official access to God who prescribes these systems to the common man. He or she shows us how we can "reach" God.

"If you do steps one, two and three, you can access God. Just be sure not to do A, B and C or you will be disqualified," says the religious system.

If that sounds like an accurate definition to you, then you can see the fundamental problem.

Man cannot reach God.

It is absurd to think that man could create a system that could access the Divine on his own. God is holy and we are sinners. We are disconnected from God by an unreachable chasm. There is only one way man can access God.

God has to reach out to us.

Jesus comes to us because we could never get to God on our own. There is no religious system that can bridge the divide between a sinner and a holy

God. We cannot get there on our own no matter how hard we try or how holy we think we are. That is the beautiful thing about God's gift through Jesus. He does it for us. It is only through Him that forgiveness and new life are possible.

Jesus told him, "I am the way, the truth, and the life. No one can come to the Father except through me." (John 14:6)

When you look at it that way, religion is finished. It died two thousand years ago on the cross. There is no bridge to God outside of a relationship with Jesus.

A few years back, I was leading a Bible study in my friend's apartment and we had invited a new friend we called "Big John." He was a large, rough-looking dude with tattoos and drove a semi-truck for a living. One night, we were discussing Jesus and Big John's face suddenly changed. I didn't know how to read his expression at first and I couldn't stop glancing over at him. So I finally just asked him what was wrong.

"I just realized for the first time that Jesus is God." He told everyone.

We all cheered, but the look of bewilderment didn't leave his face. He couldn't get over the fact that he had been raised in a fairly religious home, full of traditions, church and prayers, but had somehow missed the most important part: *salvation through Jesus.*

"Now that you believe, are you ready to get water

baptized?" I asked him.

"Yes. Can I bring my daughter? I want her to see this," he replied.

The next week, in a freezing cold pool outside that apartment community, we water baptized Big John in the name of The Father, The Son and The Holy Spirit. Everyone cheered in excitement as he came up out of the water ready to follow Jesus and embrace his new life.

Water baptism doesn't need to be complicated. It is the outward expression of an inward decision. It is not the water ceremony that saves you. Jesus is the Savior. Baptism is the celebration that the old is washed away, the sun has set, yesterday is behind us.

If you ask me, there is only one thing more beautiful than the sun setting on the water.

The sunrise on a new day.

9

Discussion Questions

Why is water baptism an important first step in the new life of a follower of Jesus?

According to your experience, is there a difference between *religion* and relationship?

UNcomplicate It

Have you been water baptized? What are reasons that could hold someone back from taking this step of faith and obedience?

WHAT IS CHURCH?

Before our church was ever an official "church," we were just a group of friends meeting up for dinner on Sunday nights and studying the Bible. Our motto was "Trying to follow Jesus together." About half of the group was new to following Jesus and excited to make a difference. So one night I pitched an idea I had seen before.

"What would it look like if we pooled our money together to help a whole laundromat with clean clothes for an hour? We could get the word out to our homeless friends, single parents, anyone who is struggling or under-resourced. No strings attached."

"It's about time we did something. I was getting bored just sitting around reading the Bible!"

We all laughed out loud because we knew it was true. Three people in the group had just been water baptized and it was time for something to change. After all, completely changed people, completely change the world.

Free Laundry Night was an instant hit with our friends and surrounding community. Who would have thought that helping people with free laundry service would be so fun and exciting? Before long, it became a monthly tradition. We would all meet up with quarters at the same laundromat to help as many people as we could. We met all sorts of people and made all kinds of new friends. Before long, more people were wanting to help and the laundromat was full, so we had to start looking for a second location. There was no way around it, Laundry Night was becoming our strongest tradition.

One night, I was watching our people in that laundromat loving and serving people and I had a vision of The Church. I didn't see a weekly service or someone preaching or anything that you might expect when you envision a church. I had a vision of what God sees when He sees us together like that.

I saw a family.

Family and tradition go hand in hand, as do church and tradition. When I was growing up, my family had a handful of traditions, some of which were passed down from my parents. Some we just made up on our own. One of our most memorable traditions took place on Thanksgiving. Every year, as we sat around the table eating turkey, we would take turns saying what we were most thankful for. I always loved hearing unique things for which our family was thankful and it filled the room with a grateful spirit.

Now that I am older and have a family of my own, my wife and I are carrying on some old traditions, but are forming new ones too. One of our favorites is an old tradition with a new spin on it. On Thanksgiving afternoon, when we are all full from a big meal, we take sleeping bags out to the backyard and lay out on the trampoline together. We stare up at the sky and take turns saying what we are thankful for. The first time we did this, we were out there for over an hour! It's an old tradition with a new spin on it.

Someone recently said to me,

"I'm really disappointed I had to miss church last Sunday. I was really looking forward to learning how to take Communion right."

(Communion is also referred to as the Lord's Supper or Eucharist.) How a church celebrates Communion is always a strong tradition in church. I hear this a lot because people come from all sorts of different faith backgrounds and practices that all "do church" differently.

Traditions change over time because it is too easy for the original significance to get lost to the next generation. Sometimes, if you want to keep the tradition alive, you just need to contextualize it — put your own spin on it. The important thing is that it honors the creator of the tradition and its purpose. Even Jesus, when He was with His disciples for His last supper, was actually forming a new version of a previous tradition that took place during the Jewish

Passover.

Jesus said, "I have been very eager to eat this Passover meal with you before my suffering begins. For I tell you now that I won't eat this meal again until its meaning is fulfilled in the Kingdom of God." Then he took a cup of wine and gave thanks to God for it. Then he said, "Take this and share it among yourselves. For I will not drink wine again until the Kingdom of God has come." He took some bread and gave thanks to God for it. Then he broke it in pieces and gave it to the disciples, saying, "This is my body, which is given for you. Do this in remembrance of me." After supper he took another cup of wine and said, "This cup is the new covenant between God and his people—an agreement confirmed with my blood, which is poured out as a sacrifice for you." (Luke 22:15-20)

As a pastor, I continue to grow more convinced that there is no right or wrong way to "do church." The important thing is that we honor the One who created it and the purpose which He had in mind.

Maybe you see church as something old and crusty that was passed down from a previous generation or maybe you are a part of forming something new. Whatever your experience, God sees the gathering of His people as a family and He isn't nervous when you contextualize that experience to help you engage God and His people.

In fact, "putting your own spin on it" may be the oldest tradition of them all.

Discussion Questions

Did you have any special family traditions growing up? What was your favorite part?

Why is it important that we never lose the tradition of Communion? What is its purpose?

UNcomplicate It

If God's church is like a family, where do you find yourself?